GALE
CENGAGE Learning

Novels for Students, Volume 26

Project Editor: Ira Mark Milne

Editorial: Jennifer Greve

Rights Acquisition and Management: Margaret Chamberlain-Gaston, Leitha Etheridge-Sims, Kelly Quin, Tracie Richardson **Manufacturing**: Drew Kalasky

Imaging and Multimedia: Lezlie Light **Product Design**: Pamela A. E. Galbreath, Jennifer Wahi **Vendor Administration**: Civie Green

Product Manager: Meggin Condino

For more information, contact
Gale
27500 Drake Rd.
Farmington Hills, MI 48331-3535

of the editors or publisher. Errors brought to the attention of the publisher and verified to the satisfaction of the publisher will be corrected in future editions.

ISBN-13: 978-0-7876-8683-3
ISBN-10: 0-7876-8683-2
eISBN-13: 978-1-4144-2933-5
eISBN-10: 1-4144-2933-9
ISSN 1094-3552

Printed in the United States of America
10 9 8 7 6 5 4 3 2 1

The Killer Angels

Michael Shaara 1974

Introduction

The Killer Angels (1974) covers a four-day period (June 29, July 1-3, 1863) during which the Battle of Gettysburg, the turning point of the American Civil War, was fought in Pennsylvania. Shaara describes the battle from the points of view of several of the main participants, the most important being, on the Confederate side, General Robert E. Lee, commander of the Army of Northern Virginia, and Lieutenant General James Longstreet, commander of the Confederate First Army Corps and Lee's second in command, and on the Union side, Colonel Joshua Lawrence Chamberlain, commander of the Twentieth Maine Infantry regiment. Shaara reveals the thoughts and feelings of these and other soldiers as they play out their parts in the historic battle: why they fight, what motivates them, what their beliefs are, what decisions they make and why. Through dialogue and inner monologue, the author explores the great issues of the day, including slavery, states' rights, and theories of war and how they are applied to the battle at hand, as well as religious and philosophical issues such as the role played by chance and destiny in the great battle. In vivid prose that recreates the sights, sounds, and smells of battle, *The Killer Angels* makes readers feel that they are right there in the midst of the action. *The Killer Angels* won the Pulitzer Prize for Fiction in 1975 and was the basis for the film *Gettysburg* in 1993.

Despite Faulkner's roots in the South, he readily condemns many aspects of its history and heritage in *Absalom, Absalom!*. He reveals the unsavory side of southern morals and ethics, including slavery. The novel explores the relationship between modern humanity and the past, examining how past events affect modern decisions and to what extent modern people are responsible for the past.

Author Biography

Michael Shaara was born on June 23, 1929, in Jersey City, New Jersey, the son of Italian immigrants. He attended Rutgers University and it was there that he realized his goal was to become a writer. He wrote his first published story while he was still an undergraduate, even though his creative writing teacher was less than enthusiastic about his work and suggested he aim for a more literary style.

Shaara graduated from Rutgers with a Bachelor of Arts degree in 1951 and then pursued graduate study at Columbia University (1952-1953) and the University of Vermont (1953-1954). He also began to publish science fiction short stories in popular magazines.

Shaara married Helen Krumweide in 1950, and in 1954, he moved with his wife and young son to Florida, where Shaara was for a short time employed as a police officer in St. Petersburg. After this he began to teach English, literature, and creative writing at Florida State University in Tallahassee. He was associate professor at that university from 1961 to 1973.

Shaara continued to write and published more than seventy short stories in magazines such as *Playboy*, *Galaxy*, *Redbook*, *Cosmopolitan*, and the *Saturday Evening Post*. His first novel, *The Broken Place*, about a soldier who returns home from the Korean War and becomes a boxer, was published by

New American Library in 1968.

The origins of Shaara's second novel, *The Killer Angels*, was a visit Shaara made with his family to Gettysburg, the site of the famous Civil War battle. Shaara worked on the manuscript for seven years, only to see it rejected by fifteen publishers. It was finally accepted by a small independent publisher, the David McKay Company, and published in 1974. It did not attract great attention from reviewers, but this did not prevent it from being awarded the Pulitzer Prize for Fiction in 1975. The novel was the basis for the 1993 television miniseries *Gettysburg*.

During a difficult process of recovery following a serious motorcycle accident, Shaara continued to dedicate himself to his writing. His third novel, *The Herald*, was published by McGraw in 1981. It is about a scientist who wants to create a master race and plans to kill millions of people in order to accomplish his goal.

The following year, a selection of Shaara's previously published short stories, *Soldier Boy*, was published by Pocket Books.

During the 1980s, however, Shaara's health was in decline. He had already, in 1965, suffered a major heart attack, and on May 5, 1988, in Tallahassee, he died of a second heart attack.

After Shaara's death, his children discovered an unpublished manuscript by their father. Called *For Love of the Game*, it is a story about an aging baseball pitcher. It turned out that during the 1980s,

Shaara had tried but failed to find a publisher for this novel, which was eventually published in 1991 by Carroll & Graf. In 1999, *For Love of the Game* was released as a major motion picture by Universal Studios.

Media Adaptations

- *The Killer Angels* was adapted by Turner Pictures and aired as the television miniseries *Gettysburg*, in 1993.

- The novel was also recorded, in an unabridged audio version by Books on Tape and published in 1985.

Foreword: June 1863

The Killer Angels begins with a foreword that sets the scene for the action that follows. It is divided into two sections. The first section describes the two armies. The Army of Northern Virginia, consisting of seventy thousand men commanded by Robert E. Lee, has on June 15, 1863, crossed the Potomac at Williamsport and invaded the North. Its aim is to draw the Union army out into the open and crush it. In late June, the Union army, the Army of the Potomac, numbering eighty thousand men, turns north to begin its pursuit of the rebels that ends at Gettysburg. The second section of the foreword briefly describes the main characters: on the Confederate side, Robert Edward Lee, James Longstreet, George Pickett, Richard Ewell, Ambrose Power Hill, Lewis Armistead, Richard Brooke Garnett, J. E. B. Stuart, Jubal Early; on the Union side, Joshua Lawrence Chamberlain, John Buford, John Reynolds, George Gordon Meade, Winfield Scott Hancock.

Monday, June 29, 1863

1: THE SPY

Harrison, a spy sent by Longstreet from Virginia to locate the position of the Union army, looks down from a high position in the woods upon two Union corps, twenty thousand men moving fast. He slips away on horseback and reaches Confederate headquarters after dark. He is taken to General Longstreet and to whom he gives detailed information about the position of the Union army. Longstreet did not even know that the Union army was on the move and certainly not as close as two hundred miles away. He is skeptical about the accuracy of Harrison's report, but Harrison insists he is right. Longstreet knows that if Harrison's information is correct, his army is in great danger, with the Union army so close. He takes Harrison to see Lee, who is doubtful whether he should make a move on the word of a spy. But he does decide to move quickly, aiming to get behind the Union forces and cut them off from Washington. Lee gives the order to move at dawn in the direction of the small town of Gettysburg.

2: CHAMBERLAIN

Colonel Joshua Chamberlain, commander of the Twentieth Maine regiment, is awakened by his aide Buster Kilrain. Kilrain informs him that they are being sent 120 mutineers from the Second Maine regiment, men who have refused to serve the final year of their three-year enlistment. There is a message signed by General Meade, the new Union commander, to the effect that these men are to fight. If they refuse, Chamberlain is authorized to shoot them. The ragged, tired mutineers are presented to Chamberlain by a captain from a Pennsylvania regiment. Chamberlain allows their leader, Joseph

Bucklin, to express their grievances. Bucklin complains about the incompetence of the officers they have served under. After Chamberlain receives orders to move west into Pennsylvania, he gives what he hopes will be an inspirational speech to the mutineers about the cause of freedom they are fighting for. He says he needs them because the regiment is under strength, but he will not shoot them if they refuse to fight. As the regiment moves in the direction of Gettysburg, Chamberlain is pleased to hear from his brother Tom that all but six of the mutineers have agreed to fight.

3: BUFORD

At noon, from the top of a hill outside Gettysburg, Union commander John Buford observes rebel troops on the far side of the town. There is at least a brigade, but no cavalry in sight. Buford has two brigades with him; the big infantry is a day's march behind him. Buford watches as the rebels withdraw then sends scouts to gather information about the rebels' movements so he can know what the Union forces are facing. Next, he sends a message to John Reynolds and General Meade explaining that he expects the rebel army to be there in force in the morning. He worries that they will occupy a strong position in the hills, and he does not know whether his forces will be able to hold their ground until Reynolds arrives with his infantry. After dark, the scouts return and report that the whole Confederate army is on its way to Gettysburg. Later, Buford receives a note from Reynolds, who promises to come in the morning as early as possible.

4: LONGSTREET

In Longstreet's camp, thirty miles from Gettysburg, Longstreet worries because he does not know the position of the Union army. He was expecting to hear from General Stuart, who has been gone for several days but has sent no information. General Hill disbelieves reports of Union cavalry in Gettysburg, and Lee accepts Hill's judgment. Longstreet is not so sure. General Pickett, an old friend of Longstreet's, arrives. Pickett and his forces are bringing up the rear; he is desperate to see some action and asks Longstreet if he can be moved forward. Longstreet tells him his time will come. Longstreet then talks to Armistead, who is confident of victory in the forthcoming battle. They discuss military strategy, including the merits of offensive and defensive war. Other officers discuss why the war is being fought. Just before dawn, Confederate soldiers approach a Union picket, and one of the pickets fires the first shot of the battle.

Wednesday, July 1, 1863: The First Day

1: LEE

Lee arises at dawn. He has heart trouble and does not feel well. His aide Major Taylor informs him that nothing has been heard from Stuart. He also informs Lee of Hill's skepticism about the presence of Union cavalry at Gettysburg. Lee knows that if cavalry is present, there will be infantry close by. He tells Taylor that he does not want to fight until his entire army is concentrated. Lee deals with some civilians and consults further with his aides. Marshall wants to court-martial Stuart for his continued absence, but Lee offers him no support. Longstreet arrives, and Lee tells him to stay in the rear, since he cannot afford to lose him. They discuss tactics; Longstreet favors defense, but Lee wants to attack. When the army gets on the move, Lee and Longstreet ride several miles together. At about ten in the morning, they hear the first sounds of artillery in the distance.

2: BUFORD

At dawn, Buford deals with the first rebel attack and expects another more organized one imminently. His forces are dug in and he is confident, but he writes to Reynolds saying he expects relief. Another rebel attack is repelled, and prisoners are taken. Buford knows that the rebels are there in force, and the Union position is precarious against such numbers, even when Reynolds arrives. When the big attack comes, Union lines are tested, and Buford considers pulling out. Then Reynolds arrives with two corps of fresh Union infantry, and their prospects look good. But when Buford and Reynolds ride out together, placing their troops, Reynolds is shot and killed.

3: LEE

Lee has issued orders to Heth not to force a major engagement. He frets about not having heard from Stuart and, therefore, not knowing the disposition of Union forces. He soon realizes that Heth has taken on more than he can handle and has been repulsed. Heth arrives and explains that he was surprised by the presence of Union infantry. He thought he was faced only by local militia. He apologizes. Rodes and Early continue the attack, and Heth requests permission to do so also. Lee is unsure but then tells Heth to go ahead and tells Pender to do the same. The battle rages. Heth is wounded, but then a courier from Early brings the news that the enemy is falling back. Lee instructs Early to take Cemetery Hill, unless he is faced with a superior force, since he does not want Union forces established on high ground. Longstreet arrives, and he and Lee disagree over tactics. While Lee wants to press the attack, Longstreet wants to disengage, swing the army round, and get a good defensive position on high ground between the Union army and Washington, so that Union forces will have no option but to attack. Lee is worried that he sees no sign of an assault on Cemetery Hill. Longstreet again pushes for withdrawal, but Lee says he will attack the next day if Meade is there with all his forces.

4: CHAMBERLAIN

Chamberlain and the Twentieth Maine make their way north across the Pennsylvania border to Hanover. Tom Chamberlain, Joshua's younger brother, teaches one of the men from Second Maine the regiment's bugle call. Chamberlain reflects on the battle of Fredericksburg, in which he participated; the characteristics of Maine; his mother and father; his home. When they reach Hanover, the townspeople are delighted to see them. As evening comes they go to rest; they have marched a hundred miles in five days. But soon they hear their bugle call and are ordered to march on through the night to Gettysburg; they hear rumors about the battle that has just taken place and also the false information that the popular General McClellan is back in charge of the Union army. They reach Gettysburg at midnight.

5: LONGSTREET

In the evening after the first day of battle, Longstreet rides back from Gettysburg to his camp. He knows that Lee will ignore his advice and attack in the morning. He thinks back to the previous winter, during which his three children died of fever. He discusses the day's events with the Englishman, Fremantle, who is there as an observer of the battle. Fremantle speaks of his admiration for Lee and his hope that England will ally itself with the Confederacy. Longstreet relates some memories of Stonewall Jackson, the Confederate general who was killed before Gettysburg, and argues the case for defensive rather than offensive war.

6: LEE

That evening Lee receives congratulations for the Confederates' success in battle. Ewell explains that he did not attack Cemetery Hill, because it did not seem practical. Early, to whom Ewell defers, confirms the reasons for their decision. Lee explains

Longstreet's preferred strategy, but Ewell and Early favor attack rather than defense. Lee rides off and encounters General Trimble, who is angry with Ewell for not attempting to take the hill. He believes it could have been done. Lee returns to his headquarters, where Ewell apologizes for being too careful during the battle. Lee realizes Ewell is not up to the task, but he speaks kindly to him. Alone later in the night, Lee resolves to attack the following afternoon.

7: BUFORD

At two o'clock in the morning, Buford rides along Cemetery Hill as his men dig in. He is in pain from an arm wound. He goes to a farmhouse where officers are gathered and sees two majors arguing about who is in charge. Buford learns that Howard, who was in charge of the Eleventh Corps that did not perform well, has complained that Buford did not support Howard's right flank. Buford explains to Hancock how much he was involved in the previous day's action. Meade arrives. Buford has received his orders, cannot get close to Meade, and rides back towards the cemetery, where he talks to the dead Reynolds, saying that they held the ground.

Thursday, July 2, 1863: The Second Day

1: FREMANTLE

At three o'clock in the morning, Fremantle eagerly awaits the coming battle as he joins the other officers at breakfast. He feels at home, thinking of the Confederate army as transplanted Englishmen. He is certain they will win. The officers observe the Union lines through field glasses. A bit later, Fremantle rides with Longstreet then goes off to talk with some of the European officers; he thinks about how he supports the traditions of the South rather than the democracy favored by the North.

2: CHAMBERLAIN

Kilrain informs Chamberlain that just before dawn they found a wounded black man. Chamberlain has rarely seen a black man before. They cannot communicate with him and think he must have been a slave who tried to run away from the Confederates and was shot. They feed him and treat his wound. They conclude he has not long been in the country. It later transpires that he was shot by a woman in Gettysburg after he came into town looking for directions. Bugles blow and the division forms itself. Colonel Vincent informs Chamberlain that they will probably be held in reserve that morning. The call comes to advance, and the corps begins to march. Then they are ordered to stop, and they rest in a field. Chamberlain talks with Kilrain about black people; Chamberlain says that he sees no essential differences between the races, only the humanity and the "divine spark" they share. He regards slavery as a terrible thing. Chamberlain sits against a tree, waiting for the battle to begin.

3: LONGSTREET

Lee seeks Longstreet's agreement on tactics. He points out that neither Ewell nor Early favors withdrawing. They believe they can take Cemetery Hill and Culp's Hill, which are held by Union forces. Poring over a map, the generals plan their moves as Lee gives orders. Johnston is given responsibility for moving Longstreet into position, and Longstreet insists that his men are not seen by the enemy. Johnston confesses he knows little about the roads, which causes Longstreet to curse at the continued absence of Stuart, who would have been able to supply information. They begin the march at noon. Lee and Longstreet ride together; they recall past battles, and Lee hopes the coming one will be the last. After Lee rides off, Johnston informs Longstreet that if they continue their present course, they will be seen by the enemy. Furious, Longstreet orders a change of direction. They find another route, but Longstreet knows that the extra march will tire his men. When they reach the front, they unexpectedly find Union soldiers in the peach orchard. Hood wants to shift the plan and go right, behind the Big Round Top. He says otherwise he will lose half his division. Privately, Longstreet agrees this is the wisest course but refuses to deviate from Lee's orders. The attack begins.

4: CHAMBERLAIN

Chamberlain hears artillery fire and knows the battle has begun. It is nearly 4 p.m. Vincent informs them that the rebels are attacking the Union left flank and places Chamberlain's regiment on Little Round Top, the extreme left of the Union line. He instructs him to hold the line at all costs. Chamberlain places his men; he can see the battle raging below. Three of the Maine mutineers agree to join the fight. The rebels come in full force, and the Union line holds. The rebels come again. There are many dead on both sides; Kilrain is wounded, and Chamberlain is wounded in his right foot. He continues to direct his forces effectively, but they are running low on ammunition, and the rebels are still coming. He directs his brother Tom to fill a gap in the line. One man says they cannot hold the line and should pull out. Chamberlain refuses. He orders his men to fix bayonets, and they charge down the hill, routing the rebels and taking five hundred prisoners. Kilrain is wounded for the second time, but he saves Chamberlain's life by shooting a rebel who was aiming his rifle at Chamberlain. Tom brings news that they fought off four rebel regiments, perhaps two thousand men. The Twentieth Maine takes 130 casualties, which is nearly half the regiment. Chamberlain feels great joy at the victory.

5: LONGSTREET

In the evening, Longstreet visits the wounded Hood in the hospital. Then he learns from Sorrel that Hood's officers blame Longstreet for the failure to take the hill. Longstreet knows that no one will blame Lee, even though they were following Lee's orders. Longstreet learns that Hood's division suffered losses of 50 percent and knows they no longer have the resources for another major assault. Then he hears that General Pickett has arrived with five thousand fresh men. He goes to headquarters to talk to Lee and finds that at last Stuart has returned. Lee tells Longstreet they almost succeeded, but Longstreet knows that is not true. He informs Lee that there are three Union corps dug in on the high ground. When Longstreet moves off into the crowd he sees Marshall, who wants to court-martial Stuart but says Lee refuses to sign the papers; Longstreet says he will speak to Lee about it. He rides with Fremantle, who is full of praise for Lee, but Longstreet speaks of Lee and his tactics in a way that he immediately realizes might be thought disloyal. He returns to camp and listens to the officers singing, drinking, and telling stories. An emotional Armistead recalls a time back in 1861 when he sang a particular song with his close friend Win Hancock, who is now on the opposing side.

6: LEE

Lee works all night. He reflects on why he had to break his vow to defend the Union; he feels he had no choice, since he could not take up arms against his own people. He now has to decide whether to move to higher ground in another place or stay and fight. Stuart visits him; Lee rebukes him for letting the army down, and Stuart offers to resign, but Lee says he needs him in the coming fight. Lee decides he must attack. He plans to use Pickett's forces in a drive to the center of the Union line that will split the enemy in two, and then he wants to use Stuart's cavalry at the rear to complete the rout.

Friday July 3, 1863

1: CHAMBERLAIN

At dawn, Chamberlain climbs a tree and surveys the scene. His foot is still bleeding, and the men are out of rations. He thinks the rebels will come again that day; he has only two hundred men left, but they are in a good position. The battle has begun, to the north of them, on the opposite flank. An aide from Colonel Rice arrives and tells Chamberlain he is relieved; Colonel Fisher is to take over their position. Chamberlain does not want to leave, and the Union lieutenant takes them to their new position, which is right in the center of the Union line.

2: LONGSTREET

Longstreet and Lee ride together; Longstreet says he has discovered a way south and wants to move, but Lee will hear none of it. He explains his attacking strategy. Longstreet protests, saying a frontal assault will be a disaster. Lee insists there is no alternative. Word comes that Union forces are attacking Ewell. Lee is surprised. Lee talks to Wofford, who tells him his men cannot break the Union lines because the enemy has brought in reinforcements. Lee still believes that his fifteen thousand men can do it. The plan is for a heavy artillery barrage on the center of the Union line, followed by a charge at the center by Pickett's division, which will break the line. Longstreet says he believes the attack will fail. They will have to march for a mile over open ground under constant artillery fire. Lee, however, is confident of victory. Longstreet says nothing about his doubts as he explains the battle strategy to the officers, including Pettigrew, Trimble, and Pickett. Longstreet waits for the 140 guns to begin firing and for the Union reply. It will be the greatest artillery barrage ever fired.

3: CHAMBERLAIN

Lieutenant Pitzer guides Chamberlain and his men to their position, near Meade's headquarters. They are to be held in reserve. Chamberlain is called over to meet General Sykes, who is impressed by what he has heard of Chamberlain's bayonet charge. Sykes promises he will get rations to Chamberlain's men. Chamberlain walks back to his men, troubled by his injured foot. Tom reports that Kilrain has died not from his wounds but of a heart attack. The artillery battle begins, and shells fall very close to Chamberlain and Tom. Chamberlain sleeps intermittently while he waits for action.

4: ARMISTEAD

Armistead watches the artillery barrage begin just after one o'clock in the afternoon. He sees Pickett writing a poem for his sweetheart and gives him a ring from his finger to send to her. Pickett is joyfully awaiting the action. Garnett rides up on horseback and says he intends to ride into the battle, even though that is against orders. His leg is injured, and he cannot walk. Armistead tries to get Pickett to order Garnett not to make the charge, but Pickett refuses. The artillery barrage slackens, and the Confederates begin their charge, moving through the woods and then into the open fields beyond. Armistead encounters Garnett still on horseback and knows he will die. The Union artillery opens up once more, and a wave of fire rolls down on the advancing men who form a line a mile long. Many men fall, and the gaps in the line are closed up. Armistead permits himself to hope that they may succeed. They face devastating canister fire— millions of small metal balls. Armistead yells encouragement to Kemper. He is wounded in the leg, but he still goes forward and manages to reach the stone wall that is the object of their charge. He is hit in the side and knows he is dying. The dead are all around him, most of them Confederate soldiers. He asks a Union officer if he can send a message to his old friend General Hancock. He is informed that Hancock is wounded; he prays that Hancock may survive, then he dies.

5: LONGSTREET

Longstreet sits watching the battle and then sees his men retreat. He orders Pickett to retreat. He thinks that all his men have died for nothing. Lee appears, and the retreating men slow at the sight of him. Longstreet thinks he will never forgive Lee. Lee says he expects a counterattack, but the Union troops pull back. Longstreet rides back towards the camp. He learns that of the thirteen colonels in

Pickett's division, seven are dead and six wounded. Lee tells Longstreet they must withdraw that night. He says they will do better next time, but Longstreet disagrees. Lee admits he was wrong in his battle strategy and that Longstreet was right.

6: CHAMBERLAIN

In the evening, Chamberlain goes off to be on his own. He looks over the battlefield. Tom joins him and remarks on the courage the rebels showed. Tom does not understand how they could fight so hard for slavery. Chamberlain feels pity for the dead men whose corpses are being laid out on a nearby field, but he feels a thrill at the thought of fresh battles to come.

Afterword

A brief Afterword describes what happened to some of the main characters in the months and years after the great battle.

Brigadier General Lewis A. Armistead

Brigadier General Lewis A. Armistead is one of Pickett's brigade commanders. He is a shy, courtly, honest man, with a strong sense of duty. A widower, he is nicknamed Lo (short for Lothario) as a joke. He is a close friend of General Hancock, who is now fighting on the Union side, and this gives Armistead much cause for reflection. He had once said to Hancock, "if I ever lift a hand against you, may God strike me dead." He takes part in Pickett's charge, against positions defended by Hancock, and is killed.

Major General John Buford

Major General John Buford is a tall, blond cavalry soldier, born in Kentucky. He is a veteran of the Indian wars in the west and many Civil War battles. He tends to proceed slowly and carefully. Conscious of class divisions, he does not care for "gentleman" Confederates. Buford is a professional soldier who has acquired the latest weaponry for his men and taught them how to dig in and hold off any force for a while. Once he held off Longstreet's army for six hours, and he is proud of the fact that they hold their ground against the first wave of

Confederate attacks.

Colonel Joshua Lawrence Chamberlain

Colonel Joshua Lawrence Chamberlain commands the Twentieth Maine regiment with distinction. He is not a career soldier or politician; before the war he was a professor of rhetoric at Bowdoin University. He is tall, with "a grave boyish dignity," and he has a gift for making speeches. Chamberlain is always concerned with the welfare of his men and leads by example. He treats even the mutineers well, feeding them, listening to their grievances, and explaining to them the cause for which they are being asked to fight. He speaks to them in the same calm, pleasant manner that he used to deal with rebellious students. It is because of Chamberlain's decent attitude that most of the mutineers agree to fight. Chamberlain would not shoot them even though he is authorized to do so. He is also chivalrous to captured prisoners, on one occasion offering his own water flask to a rebel who requests water.

Chamberlain is a strong believer in the Union cause. He believes in the dignity of man and the equality of all men, and he has faith in the United States and in the individual. He loves his brother Tom, but he is willing to put Tom in harm's way when necessary because of his belief in the cause. Chamberlain loves army life; he finds it "a joy to wake in the morning and feel the army all around you and see the campfires in the morning and smell the coffee." He feels exhilarated after the victory that follows the bayonet charge; his ordering of the charge shows his ability to instinctively do the right thing in an emergency. After the final battle of Gettysburg is over, he is eager for future battles.

Lieutenant Tom Chamberlain

Tom Chamberlain is Joshua's younger brother. He has been recently promoted to lieutenant, and he is Chamberlain's aide. He practically worships his older brother.

Major General Jubal Early

Major General Jubal Early is the commander of one of Ewell's divisions. He is "a dark, cold, icy man, bitter, alone." Longstreet dislikes him.

Lieutenant General Richard Ewell

Lieutenant General Richard Ewell is the commander of the Union's Second Army Corps. He has "the look of a great-beaked, hopping bird. He was bald and scrawny; his voice piped and squeaked like cracking eggshells." He lost a leg in an earlier battle and has just returned to the army. Ewell has been a good soldier, but he is not a success as a commander. He is too cautious and unsure of himself and defers to the judgments of Early. He apologizes to Lee for failing to attack Cemetery Hill on the first day of battle. Lee realizes that appointing him as a corps commander, in charge of twenty thousand men, was a mistake.

Lieutenant Colonel Arthur Lyon Fremantle

Lieutenant Colonel Arthur Lyon Fremantle is an Englishman who is present with the Confederates at Gettysburg as an observer. Described as "a scrawny man, toothy, with a pipelike neck and a monstrous Adam's apple," Fremantle is an officer of the British Coldstream Guards. He admires Lee and the Confederacy because their respect for tradition reminds him of England.

Brigadier General Richard Brooke Garnett

Brigadier General Richard Brooke Garnett is Pickett's brigade commander. He is a man who has something to prove, since Stonewall Jackson accused him of cowardice. This seems to have been a false accusation, since Garnett is respected by his fellow officers, including Longstreet and Armistead. He insists on riding into battle during Pickett's charge, even though he is wounded and cannot walk. He has to prove his honor and his courage. He is killed during the assault.

Major General Winfield Scott Hancock

Major General Winfield Scott Hancock is the commander of Second Corps. He is known as an excellent soldier. Longstreet thinks of him as "dashing and confident," and Chamberlain, when he sees him, observes that he is "tall and calm, handsome, magnetic." An old friend of the Confederate Armistead, Hancock is wounded on the third day of the battle, but he recovers.

Harrison

Harrison is the Confederate scout, or spy, sent by Longstreet to report on the position of the Union army. He is distrusted by the Confederates, who treat him with disdain. By profession, Harrison is an actor.

Major General Henry Heth

Major General Henry (Harry) Heth is a commander of one of Hill's divisions. He is "a square-faced man, a gentle face." On the first day of battle, he gets into a major fight with Buford's forces, even though he was under orders not to start a major engagement.

Lieutenant Colonel Ambrose Power Hill

Lieutenant Colonel Ambrose Power Hill has recently been put in charge of the Confederate Third Army Corps. He is a "nervous, volatile, brilliant man" and was a superb division commander, but Lee has his doubts about whether Hill will be as effective now that he is in command of an entire corps.

Major General John Bell Hood

Major General John Bell Hood, known as Sam, commands one of Longstreet's divisions. He is a "tall slim man with an extraordinary face, eyes with a cold glint in them, erect in posture even as he sat, cutting a stick." He is a competent soldier.

Major General Oliver O. Howard

Major General Oliver O. Howard is the commander of the Union's Eleventh Corps that does not perform well on the first day of battle. Howard allows his line to be broken as he had also done at the battle of Chancellorsville. Hancock takes command and reforms Howard's men, after which men go to him rather than Howard for orders. This greatly angers Howard who outranks Hancock.

Brigadier General James Kemper

Brigadier General James Kemper serves under General Pickett. Formerly, he had been Speaker of the Virginia House. He is wounded in the Confederate charge on the last day of the battle.

Private Buster Kilrain

Private Buster Kilrain is an aide to Chamberlain. He is much older than Chamberlain and is described as "a white-haired man with the build of an ape." He has a fatherly attitude toward Chamberlain, and Chamberlain depends on him. Kilrain is a former sergeant who was demoted for striking an officer when drunk. He is twice wounded in battle, saves Chamberlain's life by killing a man who was taking aim at Chamberlain, and finally dies of a heart attack.

General Robert E. Lee

General Robert E. Lee is the commander of the Army of Northern Virginia. He is fifty-six years old and is not in good health, showing early signs of heart disease. He is often weary, but his appearance is impressive: "regal, formal, a beautiful white-haired, white-bearded old man." Lee is known as an honest man and a gentleman without vices. He does not drink, smoke, gamble, or chase women. He does not complain, and he is always in control. Lee is loved by his men who regard him with respect and awe. Fremantle tells a story going round that when Lee was asleep, and the army was marching by, fifteen thousand men went by on tiptoe to ensure they did not wake him. Lee's men have faith in their commander, and this is what has made the Confederate army, up to Gettysburg, so successful.

Lee has a great deal of patience. He speaks formally to his officers and does not betray his irritation at Ewell for being too cautious, and he refuses to court-martial Stuart for letting him down. He listens calmly to Trimble as he rages against Ewell. Lee's practical nature means that he deals with the situation as it is rather than worrying about how things might have been better. His practice is to give the orders and let his men get on with the job, but he is sometimes let down by the poor performances of his officers. He does not always coordinate his orders by assembling his officers in one place, and he gives no written orders.

Lee loves Virginia and believes he had no alternative but to take up arms in the Confederate cause. Throughout the battle he shows great faith in God. He believes his strategy is the way God would have it, and he believes everything rests in the hands of God. He is prepared to take risks, and he dislikes defensive warfare. Committed to attack, he ignores Longstreet's advice to withdraw. In Longstreet's eyes, Lee appears stubborn, persisting in a strategy of attack when it is clearly doomed. However, like all the other officers, Longstreet greatly admires and respects Lee.

Lieutenant General James Longstreet

Lieutenant General James Longstreet is the commander of the Confederate First Army Corps and Lee's second in command. Longstreet "gave an impression of ominous bad-tempered strength and a kind of slow, even, stubborn, unquenchable anger." He talks and moves slowly and some of the officers regard him as not much fun. But he is acknowledged to be a magnificent soldier, and he is a brilliant man. Now that Stonewall Jackson is dead, Longstreet is regarded as "the rock of the army." He is Lee's most trusted commander and confidant. Lee respects Longstreet because Longstreet always says what he thinks and tells him the truth. In return, Longstreet respects Lee as the finest commander he has served under. However, he comes into conflict with Lee over battlefield tactics. Longstreet has invented a theory of defensive warfare, but he cannot convince his officers or Lee of its virtues. He is convinced that Lee's insistence on attack is a tragic mistake. But Longstreet is also a loyal soldier who follows orders.

The previous winter, Longstreet's three children died of fever, and he has since become more withdrawn than usual, not taking part in the poker games that he used to love. Unlike most of the officers, he is not from Virginia, and he does not feel quite at home with many of them. He thinks he does not belong. But he is an old comrade of Pickett and Armistead, from many previous military campaigns, and he is extremely fond of them both. He dislikes Stuart, however.

Major General George Gordon Meade

Major General George Gordon Meade is the recently appointed commander of the Union army. He took charge only two days before the battle of

Gettysburg begins. He is described as "Vain and bad-tempered, balding, full of self-pity." Lee expects him to be a cautious commander and is surprised when Meade attacks on the third day.

Brigadier James Johnston Pettigrew

Brigadier James Johnston Pettigrew is Heth's brigade commander. He is one of the few intellectuals in the army. When Heth is injured, Lee gives his division to Pettigrew. Pettigrew suffers a minor hand wound during the Confederate charge on the third day of battle.

Major General George E. Pickett

Major General George E. Pickett is Longstreet's division commander. He is described as "Gaudy and lovable, long-haired, perfumed." He loves adventure and romance. Pickett finished last in his class at West Point, and Longstreet regards him not particularly bright but knows that he is a fighter and can be relied upon. Pickett is an exuberant, entertaining man who knows how to tell a good story. He and his men missed out on the action at Chancellorsville and Fredericksburg, and he is desperate to see action now. He gets his wish, but his division suffers 60 percent casualties in the charge on the third day.

Major General John F. Reynolds

Major General John F. Reynolds is the commander of the Union First Corps. He is a fine soldier, giving the impression of being completely in charge of the situation. He is killed on the first day of battle.

Colonel James M. Rice

Colonel James M. Rice is the commander of the Forty-fourth New York regiment in Vincent's brigade.

Major General Daniel Sickles

Major General Daniel Sickles is the commander of the Union Third Corps. He was formerly a politician from New York, and he is notorious for having shot his wife's lover. He is nicknamed "The Bully Boy."

Major Moxley Sorrel

Major Moxley Sorrel is Longstreet's chief of staff.

Lieutenant General J. E. B. Stuart

Lieutenant General J. E. B. Stuart is a cavalry division commander on the Confederate side. He was sent out by Lee to bring back information about the movement of the Union army, but he fails to do this. Some officers want him court-martialed for his failure, but Lee, although he speaks to Stuart sternly, takes no action against him. Stuart is a flamboyant man, "carefree … languid, cheery, confident."

General Sykes

General Sykes is a general on the Union side. He is a "small, thin, grouchy man, [with] a reputation of a gentleman, though somewhat bad-tempered." He congratulates Chamberlain on his bayonet charge.

Major Walter Taylor

Major Walter Taylor is an aide to General Lee. He is already a major at the young age of twenty-four.

Brigadier General Isaac Trimble

Brigadier General Isaac Trimble is nearly sixty years old. He is a fiery kind of man who is so angered by Ewell's indecision that he refuses to serve under him any longer. He is appointed division commander under Pender and is wounded in the charge on the final day of the battle.

Colonel Strong Vincent

Colonel Strong Vincent is Chamberlain's new brigade commander. He has a good reputation and the air of a man who knows what he is doing. He is killed on the second day of battle.

Topics for Further Study

- Watch the movie *Gettysburg* and make a class presentation, using video clips, in which you discuss to what extent the main characters in the film resemble the characters as created by Shaara in the novel. Do you notice any major differences between the movie and the novel?

- Read two or three nonfiction historical accounts of the third1 day of the battle. Also study the sections in the novel in which Lee and Longstreet disagree about tactics. Then write an essay in which you discuss the different ways in which the relationship between the two men at Gettysburg has been interpreted. Do your sources give any clue as to whether the Confederate defeat was due to Lee's flawed judgment or to Longstreet's lack of support for his commander's tactics?

- Write an essay in which you analyze how the attitude toward war expressed by the participants, especially Chamberlain after the battle, and Pickett, before the final charge, differ from modern attitudes toward war. Would it be fair to say that the characters in *The Killer Angels* have a romantic view of war and battle? What role does the concept of honor and glory play in this novel? How have attitudes toward war today been altered by the experience of the United States in Vietnam and Iraq?

- Make a class presentation in which you analyze two characters from the novel, comparing and contrasting them. You may choose two characters from the same side, such as Lee and Longstreet, or from different sides, such as Longstreet and Chamberlain. You may also select less central figures, such as Buford, Armistead, or Pickett. Make sure you discuss important traits such as leadership qualities. What type of leadership does each man show?

Themes

Different Beliefs about the Cause of the War

The Union men all believe that the Civil War is about freeing the slaves in the South. They subscribe to a democratic ethos that asserts the equality of all men. This is made clear early in the novel by Chamberlain, who is probably the most idealistic character in the novel. He believes he is fighting for freedom, the right of every individual to "become what he wished to become," free from oppression by tradition or the old European-style aristocracies and royalties. He explains to the mutineers that the Union army is a different kind of army than any in the past. It does not fight for land, for king, or for booty, but with the purpose of "set[ting] other men free." For Chamberlain, the Confederacy represents a new kind of aristocracy that is perpetuating tyranny through the institution of slavery.

The Confederates, however, mock the Union belief that the war is about slavery. For them it is a matter of states' rights. As Kemper says to Fremantle, the Englishman who just seems to assume the war is about slavery, "We established this country in the first place with strong state governments ... to avoid a central tyranny." This point is echoed by the rebel prisoners who are

captured by Chamberlain's men. They insist they are
fighting for their rights, not for the continuance of
slavery. But Chamberlain is not convinced. When
he sees the wounded black man, he believes he sees
the cause of the war, the enslavement of blacks,
very clearly.

Offensive versus Defensive War

A recurring theme is the disagreement between
Longstreet and Lee over strategy. Longstreet is a
pioneer of defensive warfare, and he thinks Lee is
misguided in his insistence on attack. Longstreet
consistently argues for setting up a sound defensive
position and luring the enemy into an attack. He
tries to convince Armistead of the virtues of his
theory, but Armistead insists that neither Lee nor his
army is suited for "slow dull defense." Lee is not to
be convinced, either. He loathes the nickname of
"King of Spades," which was given to him when he
ordered tunnels dug for the defense of Richmond,
Virginia. Defensive warfare goes against his
training. He has confidence in the pride of his men;
they have been outgunned before, as they are now,
but have still won great victories. He thinks only of
attacking and getting the battle won. For Longstreet,
however, Lee's attitude is out of date. The entire
war, Longstreet thinks, is old-fashioned, with tactics
dating back to the Napoleonic era, as well as
outmoded notions of chivalry and glory. "They all
ride to glory, all the plumed knights," he thinks
bitterly as he looks at the Confederate officers. In
the end, Longstreet is proved correct, and Lee

acknowledges this to him.

On the Union side, Buford espouses theories similar to those of Longstreet. He has had much experience in the Indian Wars, and he speaks disparagingly about how ineffective is "that glorious charge, sabers a-shining" against the Indian, who will hide behind a rock and then shoot you as you go by. Putting his experience to good use, Buford has schooled his men in defensive tactics, which is how they are able to dig in and hold off the attacking Confederates until relief arrives.

Divided Friendships

The nature of the Civil War is brought home by frequent references to the fact that it has split up old friends and comrades and placed them on opposite sides in the conflict. Longstreet remembers the shock of realizing that "the boys he was fighting were boys he had grown up with." Before the war, the Confederate Armistead was close friends with the Union man, Hancock. In an emotional scene, Armistead recalls his last meeting with his friend, when after dinner at Hancock's home, they stood around the piano, singing. Now, two years later, at Gettysburg, Armistead must take part in a charge on a position defended by Hancock.

When Longstreet and Lee look back on their exploits in the U.S. war against Mexico (1846-1848), Longstreet speaks admiringly of the men who served with them, noting that "Some of them are up ahead now, waiting for us." When

Chamberlain thinks about the ethics of putting his brother in grave danger by getting him to plug a gap in the line, he reflects: "Killing of brothers. This whole war is concerned with the killing of brothers." John Gibbon, of Hancock's corps, has three brothers on the Confederate side. The emphasis on brother against brother presents an image of the United States as a family divided against itself.

God's Will, Human Will, or Chance?

Lee is a religious man who sees the hand of God at work in events: "He believed in a Purpose as surely as he believed that the stars above him were really there." When he hears news of the Confederates' victory on the first day, he thinks it was God's will and offers a prayer of gratitude. He also feels that the location of the battle at Gettysburg, even though it was not consciously planned, was nonetheless a part of the divine "Intention," even though earlier he had thought, as it became apparent that a battle was looming, "We drift blindly toward a great collision."

Just before the final charge begins, Lee says, "It is all in the hands of God." But Longstreet, with his practical, down-to-earth nature, thinks differently. After Lee's remark, Longstreet thinks, " [I]t isn't God that is sending those men up that hill." In other words, it is a human decision, one that could have been made differently. Not everything is predestined or fated to be the way it is. Humans also have responsibility.

The theme that events are working themselves out, for good or ill, according to God's will, can also be seen in the fact that Lee and other Confederate officers are troubled because they broke their oaths to defend the Union. There is a certain fatalism on the Confederate side, the idea that since they broke their oaths, and also since they invaded the North, God may have turned against them.

Style

Recurring Metaphor

The title of the book points to a metaphor that recurs in the book. Before the first battle, Buford notices in the cemetery, among the gravestones, a statue of a "white angel, arm uplifted, a stony sadness." After the first battle, Buford stops in the cemetery but cannot find the white angel. It is as if the brutality of the battle has driven away this divine image.

The metaphor recurs, but with a shift in meaning, later in the novel, when Chamberlain recalls learning a speech from Shakespeare's play,

Hamlet, in which man in action is compared to an angel. On hearing his son recite the passage, Chamberlain's father remarked, "Well, boy, if he's an angel, he's sure a murderin' angel." Chamberlain then gave a speech at school entitled "Man the Killer Angel." The image recurs after the final battle ends, when Chamberlain surveys the battlefield, sees the corpses being laid out, and thinks again of man as the killer angel. The image conveys the paradox of man: he is blessed with noble feelings and high ideals, as shown in the soldiers' devotion to a cause that transcends their individual selves. This higher aspect of man's nature links him to God; it is what Chamberlain calls the "divine spark," and yet man also has another side to his nature: He is aggressive and destructive, prepared to slaughter his own kind in terrible battles.

Music

Music is a recurring motif in the novel. The sound of military bands playing is an almost constant background to the movement of troops and the battles. As Chamberlain's men enter Hanover, a band plays the "Star-Spangled Banner"; Buford hears the Sixth Wisconsin band playing "The Campbells are Coming" as they move to take up battle positions. The music is described as "an eerie sound like a joyful wind." At Confederate headquarters, a band plays "That Bonny Blue Flag" in honor of Lee. This kind of stirring, patriotic music is designed to fill the soldiers with pride and steel their hearts for battle, but there is music of another kind that plays a key role in the novel, too. An Irish song sung by a tenor in the Confederate camp on the night before the final day of battle evokes tender emotions in all who hear it. The song is called "Kathleen Mavourneen," about the sadness of old friends when the time comes to part, whether for years or forever. The officers who hear it are deeply touched, and stillness descends on the camp. For Armistead, the song recalls the last time he was with his close friend, Hancock, who is now fighting on the Union side. Music thus creates moments of reflective sadness when men feel the pain of loss and separation. Another moment comes earlier that same night, when Longstreet hears a boy playing a harmonica, a "frail and lovely sound," and

Longstreet thinks immediately of a comrade who rode off into battle and was killed. Music can therefore fortify the men for battle, or it can sadden their hearts by making them aware of the human price paid in war.

Music is also referred to in a metaphoric rather than literal sense in the description of the battles. In the midst of battle, Chamberlain hears the incredible variety of sounds, "like a great orchestra of death"; later, another unusual musical metaphor occurs: "Bullets still plucked the air; song of the dark guitar."

The Civil War Begins

The American Civil War pitted the United States federal government, under President Abraham Lincoln, against a group of initially seven southern states (South Carolina, Mississippi, Florida, Alabama, Georgia, Louisiana, and Texas) that seceded from the Union in February 1861, and formed the Confederate States of America, under President Jefferson Davis.

The main cause of the Civil War was slavery; states' rights were also an issue. The Confederate states believed they had a right to continue slavery and to expand the practice into the territories. Citing the Tenth Amendment, they argued that the federal government did not have the power to curtail states' rights and so could not prevent slavery being exported to the territories. The South also argued that northern states were failing to honor their obligations to the Constitution by assisting slaves to escape via the Underground Railroad and refusing to enforce the Fugitive Slave Law, which required the capture and return of slaves who escaped into northern free states. The South also feared long-term changes in the demographic and political structure of the United States. The northern population was growing and would soon control the federal government, leaving the South in a permanent minority.

Compare & Contrast

- **1860s:** Advances in weaponry lead to high casualty rates during the American Civil War. Muskets are deadly at ranges of hundreds of yards; rapid-firing rifles are common, and artillery becomes more mobile and lethal.

  1970s: In the Vietnam War, the most common weapon issued to American troops is the M16A1, 5.56mm assault rifle, a gas-operated, magazine-fed rifle capable of semiautomatic and automatic fire with an effective range of three hundred meters and a practical rate of fire of sixty rpm.

  Today: U.S. troops in Iraq are equipped with M16A2 semiautomatic rifles. The maximum effective range of this weapon over an area target is eight hundred meters; for a point target, the range is 550 meters. It fires forty-five rounds per minute and can also fire 40mm grenades when equipped with a M203 grenade launcher.

- **1860s:** The United States endures its most bitter and deadly conflict. The

Civil War results in the deaths of about 646,000 soldiers. Two-thirds of the deaths are due to disease.

1970s: The Vietnam War comes to an end. In 1973, a ceasefire agreement is signed and the last U.S. forces leave Vietnam. Over 58,000 U.S. servicemen die in the war. Lasting eleven years, the war is the longest in U.S. history. In 1975, Saigon, the capital of South Vietnam, falls to North Vietnamese forces.

Today: The United States is engaged in a costly war in Iraq. As of January 2007, the United States has lost over 3,000 servicemen since U.S. forces invaded Iraq in 2003; Iraqi dead are estimated to exceed 600,000.

- **1860s:** After the Civil War ends, Lee campaigns for reconciliation between the North and South. In 1865, Lee becomes president of Washington College in Lexington, Virginia, a position he retains until his death in 1870. Lee makes a point of recruiting college students from the North as well as from the South.
  1970s: In 1975, following a vote in Congress, President Gerald Ford issues a posthumous pardon for General Lee and a restoration of his

U.S. citizenship. Ford issues a statement that the pardon corrects a one-hundred-year-old oversight in U.S. history.

Today: In 2006, *The Atlantic*, in its list of the hundred most influential Americans of all time, places Lee in fifty-seventh position, and states, "He was a good general but a better symbol, embodying conciliation in defeat."

Although abolitionist sentiment was strong in the North, the abolition of slavery was not an original goal of the federal government. The North regarded secession as an act of rebellion and initially fought simply to preserve the Union.

In the early months of 1861, the Confederacy took charge of federal forts within its boundaries, and in April, Confederate forces bombarded and captured Fort Sumter in Charleston, North Carolina. This marked the beginning of the Civil War. The North immediately moved to recapture Fort Sumter and other forts; Lincoln called for seventy-five thousand volunteers. The following month, four more states, Arkansas, Tennessee, North Carolina, and Virginia, joined the Confederacy. The Confederate capital was moved to Richmond, Virginia.

In May 1861, Lincoln blockaded southern ports, cutting off exports vital to the South. On July

21, 1861, the Confederate army fought off Union forces at the first Battle of Bull Run. The following year, the war intensified. The Union Army of the Potomac, under Major General George B. McClellan, attacked Virginia but was halted at the Battle of Seven Pines and then defeated by General Robert E. Lee in the Seven Days' Battles. Lee's army recorded another victory, against General John Pope's Union Army of Virginia, in the Second Battle of Bull Run in August. The Confederacy then invaded the North and fought the Union army at the Battle of Antietam, near Sharpsburg, Maryland, on September 17, 1862. The result of the battle was inconclusive, but it did have the effect of halting the invasion and prompting Lee to return to Virginia.

Confederate successes followed, with victories for Lee's army at the Battle of Fredericksburg on December, 12, 1862, and the Battle of Chancellorsville in May 1863. Lee then decided to once more invade the North.

The Battle of Gettysburg

Lee's army began its invasion on June 15. He learned on June 28, 1863, that the Union army had crossed the Potomac in pursuit, and he concentrated his forces at Cashtown, eight miles west of Gettysburg. The stage was set for the most decisive battle of the war. On the first day of fighting, July 1, federal troops were outnumbered, since not all their forces were assembled. The rebels, led by Major Generals Robert E. Rodes and Jubal Early, forced the Union army to retreat from their positions just north and west of Gettysburg to the high ground known as Cemetery Hill, south of town. Lee ordered Lieutenant General Richard Ewell to take the hill if possible, but Ewell decided not to attempt it. That night Major General George Meade arrived with two divisions and set up a strong defensive position on Cemetery Hill.

On July 2, the second day of battle, Lee ordered General Longstreet's forces, led by Major General John Bell Hood, to capture the area south of Cemetery Hill, known as Big Round Top and Little Round Top, on the Union left flank. Union forces, enduring heavy casualties, managed to hold their ground. The Federals also held their positions on Culp's Hill and Cemetery Hill, despite determined Confederate assaults by Ewell's divisions.

On July 3, Lee attempted to capture the center of the Union line on Cemetery Ridge. The assault was preceded by a heavy artillery bombardment, after which 12,500 Confederates marched three-quarters of a mile across open terrain, during which they were subject to intense Union rifle and artillery fire. This is popularly known as Pickett's Charge, although Pickett led only one of the three divisions involved; the others were led by Brigadier General James Johnston Pettigrew and Major General Isaac R. Trimble. The charge was repulsed, with Confederate forces suffering heavy casualties.

Lee regrouped his army into a defensive position, thinking that the Union forces would attack. The counterattack never came, and on July 5, Lee's army headed back to Virginia.

The Battle of Gettysburg resulted in an estimated twenty-three thousand casualties on the Union side and twenty-eight thousand on the Confederate side.

The Final Years of the Civil War

After Gettysburg, the tide turned against the South. Northern forces, under General Ulysses S. Grant, formed and executed a comprehensive strategy to destroy the Confederate army and its economic base. A series of battles forced Lee's army to retreat to the Confederate capital of Richmond, Virginia. At the Siege of Petersburg, trench warfare lasted for over nine months. In April, 1864, Richmond fell to the Union army.

Meanwhile, General William Tecumseh Sherman marched through Georgia, capturing

Atlanta in September 1864 and Savannah in December. Lee, realizing that the Confederate position had become hopeless, surrendered to Grant at Appomattox Court House on April 9, 1865.

The Thirteenth Amendment, abolishing slavery, took effect in December 1865.

Critical Overview

Published by a small independent publisher in 1974, *The Killer Angels* at first attracted little attention from major review sources. In a very brief review in *Atlantic Monthly*, Phoebe Adams notes that Shaara had taken "a novelist's liberty of invention with [selected officers'] motives and reactions." Adams concludes that the novel was "an unusual project and has worked out well, with excitement and plausibility." The reviewer for *Publishers Weekly* comments that Shaara "fashions a compelling version of what America's Armageddon must have been like." The reviewer concludes that *The Killer Angels* is "a novel Civil War buffs will relish for its authenticity and general readers will appreciate for its surefire storytelling." In *Library Journal*, Ellen K. Stoppel comments that "Although some of [Shaara's] judgments are not necessarily substantiated by historians, he demonstrates a knowledge of both the battle and the area. The writing is vivid and fast-moving."

The novel received more attention when it won the Pulitzer Prize in 1975. Edward Weeks, in a longer review in *Atlantic Monthly*, comments that "The best way to write about battle is to tell it as the men who went through it saw it and felt it, and that is what Michael Shaara has done in this stirring, brilliant interpretive novel."

When the television miniseries, *Gettysburg*,

based on *The Killer Angels*, was screened in 1993, the novel achieved popular success, reaching number one on the *New York Times* bestseller list, nineteen years after its publication. On publication in England in 1997, the reviewer for the *Times Literary Supplement* noted that the novel concentrates entirely on the battle, rather than ranging into social territory. Commenting that "the reader becomes involved in the decisions which had to be taken and the conditions of combat, harrowingly described," the reviewer concludes that the novel is a "moving, dramatic tale."

Sources

Adams, Phoebe, Review of *The Killer Angels*, in *Atlantic Monthly*, Vol. 234, No. 4, October 1974, p. 118.

Douthat, Ross, "They Made America," *The Atlantic*, Vol. 298, No. 5, December 2006, p. 74.

Review of *The Killer Angels*, in *Publishers Weekly*, Vol. 206, No. 2, July 8, 1974, p. 69.

Review of *The Killer Angels*, in *Times Literary Supplement*, No. 4916, June 20, 1997, p. 25.

Shaara, Michael, *The Killer Angels*, David McKay, 1974.

Stoppel, Ellen K., Review of *The Killer Angels*, in *Library Journal*, Vol. 99, No. 15, September 1, 1974, p. 2092.

Weeks, Edward, "The Peripatetic Reviewer," in *Atlantic Monthly*, Vol. 235, No. 4, April 1975, p. 98.

Further Reading

Chesnut, Mary, *Mary Chesnut's Civil War*, Yale University Press, 1993.

> Wife of a Cabinet member under Jefferson Davis, Chesnut describes the Civil War, much of which she witnessed. She was in Charleston during the firing on Fort Sumter, for example, which began the conflict. The 1982 edition of this book received the Pulitzer Prize for History.

Foote, Shelby, *The Civil War: A Narrative: Fredericksburg to Meridian*, Random House, 1963, pp. 467-581.

> This is one of the best accounts of the Battle of Gettysburg written to date. It brings the personalities of the soldiers to life and clearly recreates the ebb and flow of battle as it really was, not as legend has made it.

Hartwig, D. Scott, *A Killer Angels Companion*, Thomas Publications, 1996.

> Hartwig is a historian at Gettysburg National Military Park, and in this book, he examines the extent to which Shaara's novel reflects the truth about the Battle of Gettysburg

and its key figures. He also discusses what happened to the major characters after Gettysburg.

Lewis, Clayton, "The Civil War: Killing and Hallowed Ground," in *Sewanee Review*, Vol. 103, No. 3, Summer 1995, pp. 414-25.

Lewis argues that in many respects the novel is quite conventional. Its achievement, however, is the use of modern fictional technique to convey the immediacy of Civil War combat.

9 781375 391917